WHOLE WIDE WORLD
ANGKOR WAT

by Kristine Spanier, MLIS

pogo

Ideas for Parents and Teachers

Pogo Books let children practice reading informational text while introducing them to nonfiction features such as headings, labels, sidebars, maps, and diagrams, as well as a table of contents, glossary, and index.

Carefully leveled text with a strong photo match offers early fluent readers the support they need to succeed.

Before Reading

- "Walk" through the book and point out the various nonfiction features. Ask the student what purpose each feature serves.
- Look at the glossary together. Read and discuss the words.

Read the Book

- Have the child read the book independently.
- Invite him or her to list questions that arise from reading.

After Reading

- Discuss the child's questions. Talk about how he or she might find answers to those questions.
- Prompt the child to think more. Ask: People from around the world travel to see Angkor Wat. Have you ever traveled to see a special place?

Pogo Books are published by Jump!
5357 Penn Avenue South
Minneapolis, MN 55419
www.jumplibrary.com

Library of Congress Cataloging-in-Publication Data

Names: Spanier, Kristine, author.
Title: Angkor Wat / Kristine Spanier.
Description: Minneapolis: Jump!, Inc., 2022.
Series: Whole wide world
Includes index. | Audience: Ages 7-10
Identifiers: LCCN 2021022743 (print)
LCCN 2021022744 (ebook)
ISBN 9781636903019 (hardcover)
ISBN 9781636903026 (paperback)
ISBN 9781636903033 (ebook)
Subjects: LCSH: Angkor Wat (Angkor)–Juvenile literature.
Classification: LCC DS554.98.A5 S68 2022 (print)
LCC DS554.98.A5 (ebook) | DDC 959.6–dc23
LC record available at https://lccn.loc.gov/2021022743
LC ebook record available at https://lccn.loc.gov/2021022744

Editor: Jenna Gleisner
Designer: Molly Ballanger

Photo Credits: Anton_Ivanov/Shutterstock, cover; Marti Bug Catcher/Shutterstock, 1; Emil Litov/Shutterstock, 3; Matyas Rehak/Shutterstock, 4; fototrav/iStock, 5; tsuchi/Shutterstock, 6-7; HIS Cambodia/Shutterstock, 8-9; Oleskaus/Shutterstock, 10-11; Tooykrub/Shutterstock, 12; steve estvanik/Shutterstock, 13; Adam Laws/Shutterstock, 14-15; Jixin YU/Shutterstock, 16-17; Matteo Colombo/Getty, 18; Steve Vidler/Alamy, 19; miralex/iStock, 20-21; Joss Barrett/Shutterstock, 23.

Printed in the United States of America at Corporate Graphics in North Mankato, Minnesota.

TABLE OF CONTENTS

CHAPTER 1

CITY TEMPLE

Rising above the thick forest in Cambodia is a **temple**. It is the largest religious **structure** in the world!

Make your way through the forest. Then cross a **causeway**. You are at Angkor Wat!

causeway ·····▶

Angkor Wat means "city temple." King Suryavarman II had it built in the early 1100s. He wanted a great temple for Hindu **worship**.

A **moat** surrounds the temple. It is more than three miles (4.8 kilometers) around.

DID YOU KNOW?

This area was once the center of the Khmer **Empire**. It was one of the largest kingdoms in southeast Asia.

moat

More than 300,000 people helped build Angkor Wat. It took more than 30 years! It is made of sandstone. It has three levels. They get smaller at the top.

WHAT DO YOU THINK?

Stone lasts a long time. But it is heavy and hard to move. Wood is light and easy to cut. But it falls apart over time. What materials would you use to build a structure? Why?

tower

Angkor Wat was built to look like Mount Meru. This is a mountain in Hindu **myths**. It is believed to be the home of the gods.

In the myths, Mount Meru has five peaks. The five towers of the temple stand for them. The central tower is 213 feet (65 meters) high.

TAKE A LOOK!

What are the parts of Angkor Wat? Take a look!

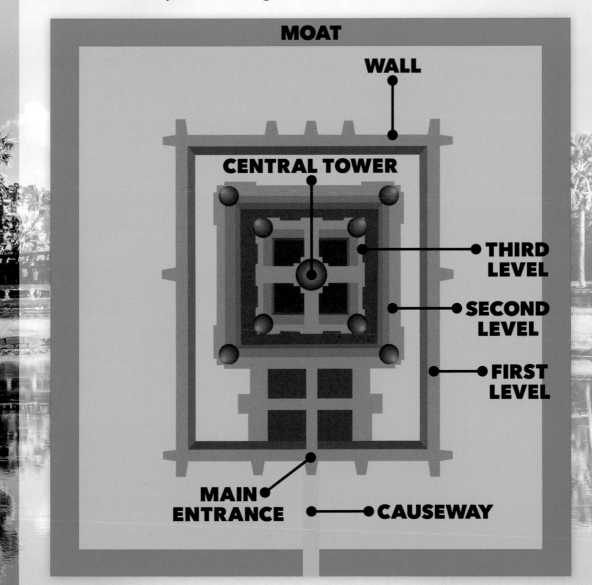

MOAT

WALL

CENTRAL TOWER

THIRD LEVEL

SECOND LEVEL

FIRST LEVEL

MAIN ENTRANCE

CAUSEWAY

CHAPTER 2

STONE ART

Over time, more temples were built nearby. People worked hard to make them beautiful. They carved pictures into the stone. Apsaras are dancing figures. More than 1,500 of them are here. No two are the same!

apsara

Some carvings show gods. Others show how people once lived.

This is the Bayon Temple. Large stone faces loom from up high. There are around 200 of them!

Another temple is Ta Prohm. The forest grew right over it. You can see carvings behind the tree roots.

WHAT DO YOU THINK?

Ta Prohm shows us what nature does when it is left alone. Do you think the trees should be removed? Why or why not?

tree roots

CHAPTER 3

ANGKOR WAT TODAY

Angkor Wat was **abandoned** in 1432. Why? People don't know for sure. But **monks** still worship here.

◄·····

Angkor Wat has become a **symbol** of Cambodia. People work to **preserve** it. They work to keep it clean.

We can all help protect Angkor Wat. If you visit, don't lean on the walls. Don't touch the stone carvings. Leave everything as you find it.

If we all do this, Angkor Wat can remain for many years. Would you like to visit?

DID YOU KNOW?

Angkor Wat is an important part of Cambodia's history. A picture of it is on Cambodia's **currency**. It is also on the country's flag.

QUICK FACTS & TOOLS

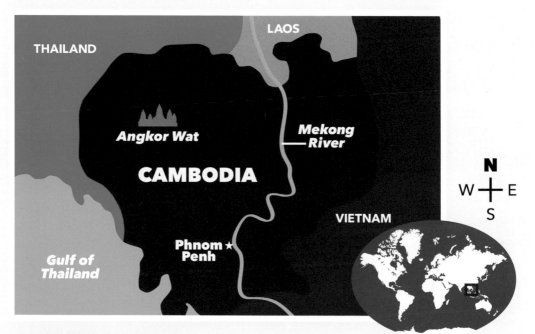

ANGKOR WAT

Location: Cambodia

Size: 400 acres
(1.62 square kilometers)

Years Built: early 1100s

Past Use: religious temple

Current Use: religious temple,
cultural site, and visitor attraction

Number of Visitors Each Year:
up to 2.6 million

abandoned: Left, never to be returned to.

causeway: A raised way across water or wet ground.

currency: The form of money used in a country.

empire: A group of countries or states that have the same ruler.

moat: A deep, wide ditch dug around a structure and filled with water to prevent enemy attacks.

monks: Men who live apart from society in a religious community according to strict rules.

myths: Old stories that express the beliefs or history of a group of people or explain natural events.

preserve: To protect something so that it stays in its original or current state.

structure: Something that has been built.

symbol: An object that stands for, suggests, or represents something else.

temple: A building used for worship.

worship: The act of showing love and devotion to a god or gods, especially by praying or singing in a religious building with others.

INDEX

TO LEARN MORE

Finding more information is as easy as 1, 2, 3.

1 Go to www.factsurfer.com

2 Enter "AngkorWat" into the search box.

3 Choose your book to see a list of websites.

FACT SURFER